GETTING NAKED WITH GOD

LaTashia M. Martin

DEDICATION

*This book is dedicated to my amazing husband (Martin), our
fantastic children(Olyvia, Monique & Austin), and my remarkable
mom (Annie Swygert). I also dedicate this book to the memory of
my daddy, Henry Von Swygert.*

ACKNOWLEDGEMENTS

Getting naked with God is only possible when I believe what HE says about ME.   "Therefore, if anyone is in Christ, the new creation has come.   The old has gone, the new is here!"
2 Corinthians 5:17 (NIV)

Table of Content

INTRODUCTION

WHAT DO YOU WANT TO BE when you grow up?** This is a question that is often asked of children as they start their paths in life and begin to discover who they are. This question is also something that hangs over the heads of many adults as they proceed through their own life journeys. Life itself is a big discovery process. You discover things about the world, other people, and most importantly, yourself. The goal of this process is to discover who you are and to use this knowledge to determine what you are supposed to be doing. Often, the journey towards this discovery becomes clouded with the ideas and choices that you make based on what you think will make you happy at that time. Sometimes where you are is not where you truly see yourself being.

If you are at a point in your life where things just do not feel right and you still feel as though you are trying to find out what you want to be when you grow up, then I say that it is time for a change. Instead of basing this change on your own ideas and choices to make you happy, it's time that you look to God for guidance.

As a Career Agent, I have had countless conversations with people who complain about their jobs or the decisions that they have made throughout life. Often, these conversations are very reactive and full of excuses as to why they are not following their passion or finding their purpose. Some people blame age, others blame the number of years spent in a job or specific occupation. Other excuses include lack of education, or the wrong education. Another theme is it is not the right time for my family. You name it; the list goes on. Many times, the excuses that people use are simply a way to cover up the root of the problem. Instead of listening to God's voice and accepting His guidance, people create their own paths and end up feeling lost. Some people will work their entire life in a career or business often feeling they were designed to do something different.; Something with a PURPOSE.

You may feel as though some of these things are true in your life right now. You picked this book up because something is missing. Like some of those people with whom I have had conversations before, you might also feel like your career consists of a whole lot of doing, but not a whole lot of being. It is time to find a career path that compliments the AUTHENTIC you.

Try looking at things from a different angle for a minute. Imagine that you have just received a career challenge, but God is the one requesting it. How would you prepare for such a challenge? You couldn't possibly just ignore it or simply say "no"! Even if you did ignore it or deny it, no matter how much you avoid the challenge or attempt to hide, sooner or later you will have to respond.

This analogy may seem a bit farfetched; especially if you have a strong personal relationship with God. You might be listening to Him daily but missing the request that He is making. "Getting naked with God" is a discovery process. This process allows you to bring yourself closer to God by putting all your insecurities and problems out on the table. The book presents a series of challenges to equip you to help you stop reacting to life but start doing what the work God designed you to do in an authentic way. It will prepare you for the changes you need to make with the assistance of others, without guilt. You can do this by being completely honest in your prayers to Him, reading His word, and truly allowing His word to transform the whole YOU.

Let me give you an example of what this means. Imagine being naked in front of a full-length mirror and having a conversation about what your body looks like with nothing covering it. The only way that you could avoid being completely honest about every lump, bump, blemish, tone, etc is if you were in serious denial. Being in denial is easy when you have clothes to cover you, but when you are naked it is hard to deny the facts. This is the same when you look at the concept of getting naked with God.

Genesis 3:10 (KJV)
And he said, I heard thy voice in the garden, and I was afraid, because I was naked; and I hid myself.

When you have an intimate relationship with God it is not the same thing. The process of getting naked is asking God to speak to you with an open mind about what His word is telling you without you debating the truth. The only way to allow this process to work is to open up to God and listen to what He is saying instead of making excuses or trying to hide the truth regarding your actions. The bible says in Hebrews 4:13, Nothing in all creation is hidden from God's sight. Everything is uncovered and laid bare before the eyes of Him to whom we must give account.

***WARNING! If this is your first time getting naked with God, you need to know that it takes time to get comfortable with this concept. The hardest part is getting undressed. Getting undressed means that you need to remove all layers of clothing. This includes limiting beliefs, past failures, and anything else that would prevent you from being your true self.

Your goal during this challenge is to see if you can listen to what God is telling you about your career and respond with your own actions. Although, the concept of getting naked with God has an emphasis on navigating your career, these concepts and principles can be used in other areas God reveals to you in the process.

You will also learn how to utilize the support of others during this challenge. In the 21day challenge, you are limited only by yourself. We will be taking a proactive approach to responding to God's call in different areas of your life, career or business. If you are up for the challenge, know that you are not alone. This challenge will provide you the opportunity to reflect and respond to the information presented.

CHAPTER *1*
Accountability is Key

That their hearts might be comforted, being knit together in love, and unto all riches of the full assurance of understanding, to the acknowledgement of the mystery of God, and of the Father, and of Christ. Colossians 2:2 (KJV)

BEFORE JUMPING INTO THIS CHALLENGE, it is critical that you get your mind right. You are   probably asking yourself how that is different than what you do every day. To hear from God clearly, you need to make sure that you mentally prepare yourself to hear from Him each day. Luke 9:23 tells us Then he said to them all: "Whosoever wants to be my disciple must deny themselves and take up their cross daily and follow me". In some cases, you may even need to be prepared to hear from Him several times a day.

You can start to open your mind to God by making a pledge and finding an accountability partner. This source can be a close friend, a mentor, or anyone who will keep you honest and ensure that what you say matches what you do. Here is your homework assignment for today.

21 Day Getting Naked with God Challenge Pledge

See to it, brothers and sisters, that none of you has a sinful, unbelieving heart that turns away from the living God. But encourage one another daily, as it is called today so that none of you may be hardened by sin's deceitfulness.
Hebrews 3:12-14

Identify an accountability partner. Ensure that this is someone that you trust to share the truth with you in love. Before you ask someone to be your accountability partner, be sure to do the following:

- Define what you need in an accountability partner
- Clearly state your expectations to them. How will they keep you accountable and how often will you meet with them?
- What will be the consequence(s) if you fail to do what you say that you are going to do? Make the result of the negative, a positive outcome. Example: if you do not follow through with what you say, then you will do something for a worthy cause. In order to be a true consequence, it must have a bit of sting to it. If you are working on your budget and you overspend, a sacrificial portion of your entertainment budget should then be donated to a ministry or an organization that you believe in.

Sample Get Naked with God 21 Day Challenge Pledge

You may want to draw up a document that looks something like this:

Your name(print): _______________________

Accountability person's name(print): _______________________

How will you be kept accountable (phone, email, text, other):_____
____
note: heavy lifting should be on the participant – NOT the accountability partner

What will be the consequence if you do not keep your commitment?

____

Clarifying Exercise
Prepare for the meeting with your accountability partner by doing a clarifying exercise and bringing this exercise to the meeting.

1.) When I stress I (example: overeat, avoid others, procrastinate)

2.) We will meet ______ times per ______ during the challenge.

Ground Rules of Accountability Partnership

- Define Rules of what accountability looks like, as partners we will create "norms" and preferences that will make the experience valuable to both of us.
- Define Consequences: if I do not do what I agree to or want to be held accountable what are the consequences. Write them and make sure they are going to have an impact that causes discomfort. Make sure they are positive but causes discomfort. For example, maybe donate a significant amount to a charitable organization that would be money taken from entertainment budget. (be creative)
- Agree on both form of communication for this process to work.

Your Name (print name)   Accountability Person (print name)

Signature   Date   Signature   Date

CHAPTER 2
Getting your mind right

ANOTHER IMPORTANT ASPECT OF GETTING **YOUR MIND RIGHT** is to focus on what God is saying through His word. This will help to make sure that you are not getting in your own way by complicating things.

Several years ago, I was in a position where I began to question my path. I couldn't understand why God had allowed me to be in a bad place with my career, thus causing me to feel unhappy. I kept trying to figure things out and to determine why things were the way they were, but after a while I finally realized that I was over-complicating things. My approach was yielding nothing until I allowed myself to take a step back and focus on God's word. I wrote a simple vision statement. "I want to talk for a living", and then found a scriptural reference to support my vision:

Habakkuk 2:2-3

Write down the revelation and make it plain on tablets so that a herald may run with it. For the revelation awaits an appointed time; it speaks of the end and will not prove false. Though it lingers wait for it; it will certainly come and will not delay.

As I reflected on those times that God did not allow things to happen for me, I realized that I was focusing on what I wanted. I was trying to play God instead of simply depending on Him.

Proverbs 3:5-6

Trust in the Lord with all your heart and lean not on your own understanding; in all your ways submit to him, and he will make your paths straight.

I wrote my vision statement and opened my ears, heart, and mind to God. I then found that by listening to Him, I was able to find my purpose. God did not only bless me with a job that enabled me to work in purpose, but He also blessed me with great co-workers and the ideal work environment for me. Not to mention, my vision was fulfilled; I talk for a living. The job I have now is the first job that I have ever had in which I am doing what I was designed to do, and the financial compensation is in alignment.

I wanted to share this story because I want you to be sure that as you are getting your mind right, you don't start to do strange things based on our own selfish motivations. It is important for you to remember that you are seeking the way in which God will get the glory from your obedience. This process can begin when you put your agenda aside. I now realize that the job that I have is something that God prepared for me when I was a young child. However, He knew that it could only be appointed to me at a time when I could appreciate such a blessing. Looking at God's word, this now makes perfect sense to me.

Ecclesiastes 3:1 NIV
There is a time for everything, and a season for every activity under heaven.

Being in a purpose-driven career and realizing that it in alignment with God's vision for me is a great feeling. It is especially great because according to Marcus Buckingham, only 2 out of 10 people do what they love. This means that only 20% of people have careers that incorporate something that they enjoy. Don't you want to be a part of this percentile?

As you are getting your mind right, you will catch yourself focusing on what YOU want and not really listening to God's purpose for your life, or what He can do for your career. That is why you must seek His word and hear from Him often during the challenge. You must not be limited by what you see as the "natural" or the "easy" way, but instead trust the process as you are mentally preparing to enter this challenge.

Isaiah 55:8-9 NIV
For my thoughts are not your thoughts, neither are your ways my ways, declares the Lord. As the heavens are higher than the earth, so are my ways higher than your ways and my thoughts than your thoughts.

Before going any further with ideas for "getting your mind right" I want you to engage in a minute exercise to help remove any limiting thoughts from your mind about where this challenge can take you. Make sure that you are in a place where you can be both mentally and physically reflective and HONEST.

Set a timer for five minutes and in the space provided, write down any reasons that come to mind as to why you cannot transform your career in 21 days. These can be any limiting factors that you feel could be impacting you. After your timer sounds the alarm, make sure that you stop right away.

Ready, Set, Write...

Look at what you wrote and circle what you believe to be the top five limiting beliefs. Transfer those words to another piece of paper and cross them out in your book.

Now….get up and go to the trash can. Rip up the piece of paper and throw it away. Let those limiting beliefs stay in the trash and exit your mind.

Now let's transition to a more positive exercise. In the box below, I want you to list 10 things that your dream job will include:

10 THINGS YOUR DREAM JOB WILL INCLUDE	

There is something powerful about writing things down but before moving forward let's reflect on what you wrote.

- How did it feel to write these things down?

- Do you believe they are possible?

- How many of these things exist in your current job?

CHAPTER 3
Self-awareness ... the truth

Ecclesiastes 4:12
*Though one may be overpowered, two can defend themselves. A
cord of three strands is not quickly broken.*

RECENTLY ASKED MYSELF, AND THEN I ASK GOD,
"what is my resistance to writing this chapter on self-
awareness for the 21-day challenge?" I wanted to know the
answer, especially since things in my career were well, and I
was finally doing parallel prenuer (which is a fancy way of
working full time with a side hustle) to get my business going.

I remember sitting in church once and hearing a story that is the
perfect summary of self-awareness. If a child said that they were
afraid of the dark, most people would accept this as a normal
response. However, imagine if that same child said that they were
afraid of the light. How would people respond to that? The initial
response might be to think that this child's statement is far from

"normal". How could someone be afraid of the light when that is where most of us spend most of our time.

For the past three and a half years, I thought I was on a journey of living more in the light because I felt like I was truly at a point where I was beyond promotion and seeking to live more in purpose. I was becoming frustrated about WHY I seemed to be at the right place in my career, but I still felt a void. I struggled with this void and the emotions that came along with it because I found myself continually thinking "Okay Lord, I am exactly where I should be, and I am SO grateful for where I am in my career, but something still doesn't feel right."

One night while sitting on my couch trying to relax (which is not something that I do often), something happened that was a breaking point for me. I am hesitant to share this story, because I feel like anyone who knows me would not believe this story. For all those who don't know me, I will be getting naked not just with God, but also with people that I don't know. However, I think sharing this story is part of my challenge. Therefore, I will fully embrace my challenge by sharing.

I had just finished arguing with my husband about spending time with the kids. I often thought, IT MUST BE NICE to have the choice to do so, but I never said it out loud. Having this internal dialogue in my head I was beating myself up far too much because at the end of the day, I DID have a choice. My choice was to do everything and did not ask for help. I had a million reasons why; he won't do it how I do, or I should not have to ask they are "OUR" children. This list and stories could continue for days.

After the argument, my husband did his normal routine which was to leave the house in order to collect his thoughts and come to terms with what had been said. I almost followed him, but I didn't. NOPE…I was too exhausted to even care that much. Later that evening, my children started arguing with each other instead of going to bed. That was my breaking point. I marched up the stairs and began screaming that no matter what I did, I was constantly treated in ways that made me feel unappreciated. I felt like every relationship in my life seemed to lack gratitude for the sacrifices that I was making.

As I continued to yell, at one point I said words I NEVER allowed my children to use I said just SHUT UP! Immediately, I could see the sadness growing in my childrens' eyes, and I felt absolutely BROKEN! I pleaded with them to go back to bed, and once they did, I found myself sitting back on the couch drowning in my own tears. Normally, when these situations arise, I cannot sleep and I usually turn to my best friend (AKA the refrigerator), but I was broken beyond my normal sadness. Therefore, my response was different. I cried out to God for an answer. I tried to watch a television show that was playing in the background, but I kept falling asleep. Finally, I gave up I shut off the television and went to bed. The emotional state that I was in at that moment is difficult to explain.

I woke up at 4:00am the next morning with God speaking these words into my spirit. "YOU ARE FAKE!" Okay God, that was not what I expected. My initial response was to go back to sleep. I wanted to stay in the dark with my clothes fully covering me, but those words resonated in my mind.

I tried and tried, but I couldn't go back to sleep. As a person who was not ready to start keeping it real, I did the most natural thing; I went to the bathroom before attempting to go back to sleep. Since I could not fall back to sleep, I decided to catch up on some emails. This seemed to do the trick, because I eventually drifted back to sleep. That didn't last long, God woke me up again to say the following:

FAKE ME + FAKE RELATIONSHIPS = UNHAPPY ME

These words rang loud in my ears. I was up now. I tried to go back into the dark and put my clothes back on, but what I had just heard now had me completely exposed. This experience was the catalyst for this chapter. I know the question you're asking because I asked the same thing. What do relationships, and my fakeness have to do with Career Transition and getting naked with God?

I will tell you the same thing that God told me. EVERYTHING!!! Over the past several months, I have been getting naked with God, and it has been a very uncomfortable experience for me. I am not used to walking around naked. When you don't have clothes on, it is very hard to lie to yourself about what you see unless you are looking into distorted mirrors.

When I first started getting naked with God, I would be naked but only look at the parts of my body in the mirror that looked good. Even though I was uncomfortable being naked, it didn't gross me out completely. I chose to look at the parts that weren't so bad. For example, I would look at my hands, calves, and legs and they looked just fine. Even though I was looking at my physical body, I also started to have conversations with God about getting naked with my life circumstances.

The areas I focused on were my career going well, my kids were all honor students, my marriage had survived fifteen years, and I had finally made a commitment to be involved with my church. Notice the order. At first, I was going to do the spiritually correct thing and shift them so that my readers didn't see that I didn't always place God first. The funny thing is that I knew better. God should ALWAYS come first. If asked, I would tell you that this is how I live my life most of the time. However, I truly believe that when I am off balance, my behavior may not always reflect that. When I don't begin my day with God, or I allow something in my life to consume me I become unbalanced. This consumption is another way of living fully clothed instead of getting naked with God. Being self-aware is an ongoing process and was not something that happened overnight for me, although I have spent my whole life in the church.

What was the problem? My life was OUT OF ORDER! Tye Trebitt said that living a life out of order is like putting money into a vending machine and expecting something to come out and it won't because it's broken. How could I minister to women as a Christian Career Agent, if my house was out of order? I believe that you cannot give God the glory if your life is not a reflection of the message.

1 Timothy 3:5 NKJV
For if a man does not know how to rule his own house how will he take care of the church of God?

When I finally took off my clothes and stood in front of a full-length mirror, I could no longer deny the years of neglect and disappointment in my reflection. It was still my little secret because I was in my closet with only a small amount of light.

To be the Authentic me during my 21-day challenge, I had to get COMPLETELY NAKED both on the inside and on the outside. Then I had to take the next step of walking out of the closet. Just like when I took off my clothes and looked at my body with disappointment, God began to unclothe emotional parts of the internal me that I had been in denial about for a long time. The first thing that I had to deal with were my priorities. They were totally misaligned.

I was able to discover these things by making a commitment to intentionally speaking to God and focus on what He was telling me by reading His word twice a day. It is also important for me to seek guidance of the Holy Spirit before calling a friend or making any conclusions regarding what I believe to be true. This was difficult in the beginning, but now I feel guilty when I don't talk to God first.

So, here is my next challenge for you. If you want to hear from God, you must first make a commitment to get in His presence at least once a day to see what He reveals to you in His word. As he is beginning to speak to you, I would challenge you to do some reflective journaling. By nature, I am not a person who enjoys the process of journaling. However, reflective journaling is something that I have been able to enjoy. You simply capture information or experiences when they happen, and then record your responses those things. If you are not familiar with the reflective journaling, go to the appendix and you will find a detailed explanation.

Before you go out and invest in a notebook, take some time and use the space below to do some reflective journaling about some of the things that you have experienced since beginning starting this book. Anytime you say Yes to God the enemy does what it does. *"The thief comes only to steal and kill and destroy;"* **John 10:10 (NIV)**

Do not skip this exercise: Take 7 minutes to really focus and be honest. The first row below is my personal information that I have included in order to give you an example. If you need some prompts for reflecting journaling you can follow my example or freestyle, the choice is yours.

Here is an example(Take some time to hear from God, and go deeper regarding what you have learned)

What did you hear from God?

What I heard from God

I am a person who lives guarded and had not really allowed myself to be vulnerable to ANY relationships. Not even to GOD!

Your Turn:

Describe your specific experience, with what you heard from God

My specific experience with what I heard from God

My lack of vulnerability guided my behavior in my marriage from day to day life to the bedroom.

I used these behaviors in a way that externally played out as a lack of trust that I justified by being guarded or didn't want to get hurt. This is starting to have a negative effect on my attitude towards work.

Your Turn:

Your Response and Specific way of testing the "story" that you told yourself
My Response and Specific way of testing my "story:"

  My husband and I were going away on a four-day get away. In the past, I never stated my expectation and allowed myself to be vulnerable or to trust that God would take care of my husband's heart if my mind was in the right place.

Your Turn:

What happened to you as a result?

My example of what happened to me as a result. Our vacation was the BEST vacation we had ever been on; even better than our honeymoon 15 years earlier. We had fun talking, dancing, and rekindling the fire…if you know what I mean! (The last statement is for the married ladies)

Because my husband and I were finally in sync with one another, my attitude at work shifted and the decisions I made were based on being Naked with God rather than my own ideas and attempts to create artificial happiness for myself.

Your Turn

CHAPTER 4
How did it feel to be physically naked with God

GETTING NAKED IS NOT AN EASY PROCESS because being undressed is very awkward. I need to warn you that being truly committed to this level of exposure allows God to have the greatest level of transformation in your most vulnerable and intimate state.

I have not always been willing to get naked with God because I have always had the ability to put on the "right" outfit or attitude to deal with the things that life used to confront me. I did this until keeping all my feelings bottled up inside began taking both a physical and mental toll on my life.

The physical impact was the first level because I used to find and still do find myself turning to food to fill an emotional or physical void. I do this instead of depending on Jesus to be my all in all. Food has become a reliable mistress that never lets me down until I look in the mirror and hit a number on the scale that exceeded my personal absolute unacceptable zone. In other words, the scale hit a number that I never wanted to see again. When I initially was writing this book, I was on a focused weight loss journey where I had separated from over 80 pounds. Although I wanted to write this as an overcomer but that is not my current reality. What I do know is that holistic health is the key not unhealthy yo-yo weight loss. Currently I work out and intentionally make better food choices. This is a much slower process but will have sustainable results.

I also have learned to love my body no matter what and be grateful for the health I have. Pause for a moment and jot down your personal perspective on your physical health.

How do you feel about your body image? Rate below
    Great   Neutral   Poor

Do you currently exercise?   YES   or   NO

Summarize other things you want to reflect on as it pertains to your physical health?

CHAPTER 5
How did it feel to be mentally naked with God

THE MENTAL IMPACT OF NOT BEING NAKED consistently spending intimate time with God had an even greater impact on the authentic me. I have learned a lot over the last six months about getting naked with God both mentally and physically. It is all about the stories that we create and tell ourselves to mask reality.

When I made a commitment this spring to mentally get Naked with God on a consistent basis, it was only because I was mentally dying inside. Even though God has placed some great friendships in my life, I didn't want to continually burden them with everything that I was dealing with. If they asked how I was doing I would put on my virtual mask and respond in a positive way. I had become a master of conversation diversion. What that means is I had a smile on the outside but suffering in silence and alone which is NOT what God wants for any of us.

Ecclesiastes 4:9-10
"9 Two are better than one, because they have a good return for their labor: 10 If either of them falls down, one can help the other up."

I was in a very dark place, but only God knew what was really going on. I started marriage counseling alone because my husband would not come with me. This was the second time that I was doing this. The first time I went to marriage counseling alone, a Pastor gave me the green light to walk away. This advice did not sit well with me because God has changed so many other situations in my life. My response was "thanks but no thanks". I knew that God could change ANY situation.

The second counselor that I worked with was a great woman who helped me on my journey into nakedness. Again, my husband would not come with me. This was the second time that I was doing this. This was a slap because I am his second wife. My insecurity stories started to run wild because he did go to counseling with his first wife, but he would not go with me. This turned out to be a tremendous blessing however, because this was a safe place for me to be completely open about things that I had never verbalized to any person. There is something incredible about the power of putting words into the "confidential air."

It was a perfect match for my "Getting Naked" process. I could discuss the negative stories that I was telling myself and shift my perspective by focusing on what God's word was revealing to me. I am also grateful that God blessed us with 3 children because I was in such a broken space mentally.

I know that was all I was fighting for at the time so if they were not in our life I would have persued divorced because of the stories that I had told myself about marriage. In my flesh, and in my selfish nature, I had every justifiable reason to walk away. I didn't even need to stay for fiscal reasons. I had a career that could maintain my lifestyle. I am also thankful that I was seeking what God said versus talking to people who may have supported my insanity.

Fast forward my husband and I have gone to marriage counseling and to be honest I think it is a resource that couples should experience. CAUTION, I highly recommend a counselor who brings in biblical perspective with their education. As believers who understand our covenant is between Christ, you and your spouse the bible should be the guiding truth.

Having God at the center when I am dealing with things like imposture syndrome, faced with difficult situations or in a place of joy. Mentally I know the foundation for all of this is spending time with God and reading what the word of God says before I go un an unhealthy mental journey.

My suggestion is that you start each morning thanking God, spending time reading scripture and prayer. It should be a requirement like brushing your teeth or taking a shower.

If you think you do not have discipline in this area I suggest hiring a Christian life coach, I did because it was another safe space for me to talk about what was going out with a person who could ask specific questions based on what the word of God said. That experience helped so much I added to my Life and Career coaching certification to gain that expertise.

Remember people who function at a level of excellence generally have a circle of support and experts to help them continue to improve.

Proverbs 11:14
"For lack of guidance a nation falls, but victory is won through many advisers."

CHAPTER 6
Getting comfortable with the uncomfortable

N JANUARY, WHEN I WAS STILL IN THE CLOSET and only dealing with surface issues, I planned a birthday celebration with my husband in Florida. Without opening old wounds, I will simply describe this as a three-day nightmare. We agreed in the airport on the way home that we would never travel alone together again.

Now…fast forward ten months. At this time, I was given another opportunity to travel with my husband alone. Initially, my mind said, "NOT GOING TO DO IT"! I quickly reminded myself that what I was doing was letting the stories that I made up in my mind guide me, and I was not relying on the God who controls and changes situations. I spent a lot of time being naked about this situation and dealing with my emotions so that I could have my mind right.

The most amazing things can happen when you honestly let go and let God. Staying in God's word really does change things. Keeping my mind on God helped me to listen to how he was guiding my life. One of the things that I learned was the power of prayer before communication. Before my husband and I went on our trip, I was clear about my expectations and he was clear about his. This was an approach that neither of us had ever taken before.

As a result, we had the best vacation ever, and the trip transformed our relationship, I already discussed this experience in greater detail, but I thought that it was important to remind yourself of the benefits of getting naked with God.

I feel closer to my husband now than I have ever felt before. I enjoy spending time with him and look forward to coming home from work every day. Take some time now and go back to the Chapter 3 exercise and dig a little deeper to reach areas in which you are starting to get naked with God and listen to what He is revealing to you.

I am not going to lie; Getting Naked is an intimidating experience. It is especially intimidating if you do it intermittently or without the word of God. That is how He speaks to you. I have discovered that the closer I want to be to God; the more barriers show up to block the desired intimacy in our relationship. However, along with the barriers come blessings

To achieve a higher level of self-awareness, you need to get Comfortable with the Uncomfortable during your quiet time with God. Over the remaining days, you will be participating in activities to constantly Get Naked with God. We will create a strategy for reflective journaling.

Don't make your plan too complicated, or you may not follow through. Some ideas could include downloading an app with a daily devotion, purchasing a devotional book, or creating an affirmation statement on why you should spend time Getting Naked with God.

Some of my favorite apps are listed below:

App	Purpose
Joyce Meyers Ministries	Daily devotion and Sermons
Jesus Calling, Sarah Young	Daily devotion
Tony Evans	Listen to Sermons
Olive Tree	App that you can purchase different bibles, a great feature is you can read bible and commentary side by side or just another version of the bible like NIV and KJV. It also syncs on all your devices(Laptop/Tablet/Phone) The specific bibles I would recommend purchasing are: NIV Zondervan Study Bible, Life Application Bible, The Message

Reminder you plan should include beginning each day reading the word. Praying for God to reveal things about you and your relationship with him.

1 John 1:6-7

If we say that we have fellowship with Him and yet walk in the darkness, we lie and do not practice the truth; but if we walk in the light as He Himself is in the light, we have fellowship with one another, and the blood of Jesus His Son cleanses us from all sin.

If you don't know where to begin with this activity, then the next model may help to jump start your thoughts. To fully benefit from the model below. Start by making a list of family members, friends, and other people in your life whose relationship can be impacted as you get Naked with God.

List of individuals who will give you the gift of feedback:

Family

Friends

Others

As you begin to spend more time reading scripture begin to ask your family, friends and other have they recognized a difference in you. BONUS, if they notice before you ask that lets you know that you are becoming more obedient to the gospel and Holy Spirit's guidance.

Up to this point you have not had to ask anyone to give you any direct feedback. If the anticipation of entering into this exercise is making you feel uncomfortable, I can completely understand.   I remember a few years back, I had and experience while preparing to be evaluated by senior managers at the company that I was working for at the time. For the first time, I was nervous about delivering training in this environment. Not that I don't get anxious, but this was a different feeling because the content had to be delivered in a very technical way. This was different from my normal style.

A wise woman pulled me to the side and said that feedback was a gift and that I should approach it as such. I would like to share that advice with you because it allows you to approach this exercise from a different perspective. She told me when receiving feedback, you should first respond like you would when you receive a physical gift. The first thing that you say is "Thank You". After saying thank you, you can do with that gift the same thing that you would do with any other gift. You can choose to do any of the following.

- *Use the gift*
- *Put the gift away for later use*
- *Give the gift someone else*
- *Throw the gift away*

The bottom line is, make sure that you are in the frame of mind to receive feedback and you should not respond to it until you can really digest the information that you are receiving. We are going to go back to your list, and then use the Johari Window model to get responses to questions that will give greater insight about who we are in four dimensions. The word "Johari" is taken from the name Joseph Luft, and Harry Ingham, who developed the model in 1955.

JOHARI WINDOW *is a model to help you become more self-aware.*

There are two key ideas behind the tool:
1.   That you can build trust with others by disclosing information about yourself.
2.   That, with the help of feedback from others, you can learn about yourself and come to terms with personal issues.

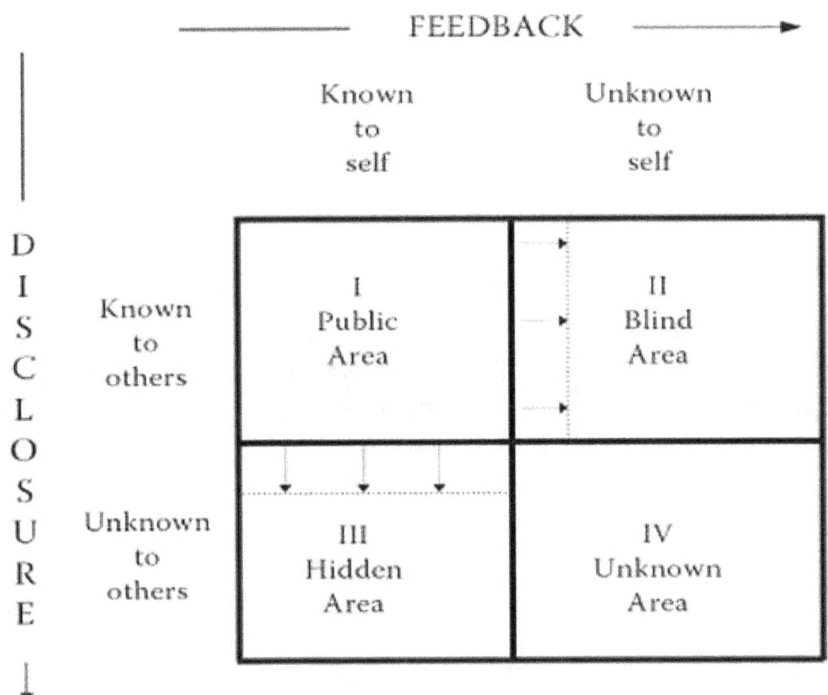

Activity: Refer to the Johari Window and respond to the information for each quadrant. This information will be used to trigger thoughts for the rest of our 21day challenge.

Quadrant I: List three things that you know about yourself that others would know

Quadrant II: Ask the individuals listed earlier in this section to give you feedback about behaviors or things that you may do that you are unaware of. This can be a challenge, but after you ask the question, do not speak or respond. LISTEN and record (you might want to record on phone) what they say in the space below:

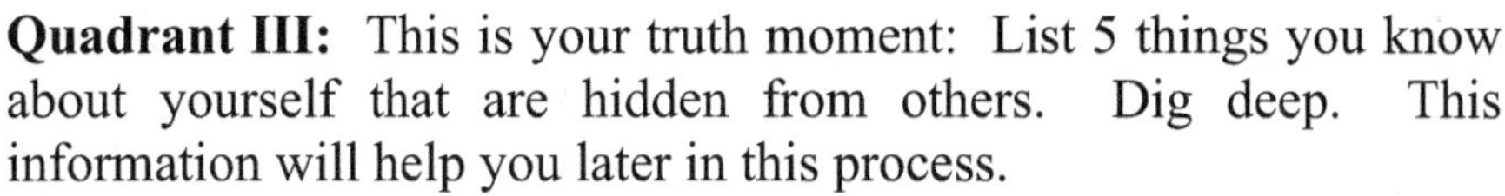

Quadrant III: This is your truth moment: List 5 things you know about yourself that are hidden from others. Dig deep. This information will help you later in this process.

Quadrant IV: As you approach this quadrant, make sure that you ask for candid/direct feedback about some things you may not have confirmed about yourself, but will explore during the 21-day challenge? When a person gives you feedback, ask for specific situations or behaviors that lead them to believe their statement. Although you are asking a second level question, do not respond to what they are saying. Just record the information below.

The Johari window model can help you build better, more trusting relationships, solve issues, and work more effectively if you are honest during the process.

Your Johari window fill in the table below with the information from previous Quadrant responses.

FEEDBACK

	Known to self	Unknown to self
Known to others		
Unknown to others		

DISCLOSURE

CHAPTER 7
Final Exercise before 21day challenge

THIS IS THE FINAL EXERCISE IN GETTING YOUR MIND RIGHT. Before you begin the 21-day challenge, I would like to give you this opportunity to review the information that you have written so far. All this information will be used as the foundation for your progress moving forward.

At this point, you should have lots of questions and information. You will explore these further on your journey to understand some of the reasons you have not been fulfilled in your current job. You may know that God has designed you for much more but feel lost and not sure where to begin answering questions that you may or may not have asked yourself.

I want to caution you that as you begin to participate in these challenges. Many of the exercises you are doing are designed to get you out of your comfort zone by having you do things that may not make sense. How you approach the activity should also give you answers about how you have been approaching life when placed in uncomfortable situations. Be open minded and honest about how the activity made you feel and have candid conversations with your accountability partner about your outcomes or things you discovered about yourself.

It is important that each day you carve out at least 30 minutes in the morning for the next 21 days. Many of the challenges should begin in the morning but you need to engage in the activities throughout the day(s). These challenges are designed to be aggressive and if you fall behind, no worries just pick back up at your rate of speed. The key is to keep doing something, the harder you work the more you will discover, and the bigger the potential payoffs will be.

If routine is a foreign concept to you, I have created a model for you to follow. Even if you like routine, I would recommend this process for you as well.

Step 1: Begin each day being grateful

Step 2: Relax and Read to hear from God by renewing your mind daily. You will find a scripture on each challenge page, but if you have your own way of spending time with God, then use that. Just make sure you are discovering what God's agenda is for your day. The only way you can hear from Him, is through His word and prayer. Take a moment to relax right now and meditate on ***Roman 12:1 (ESV).***

Romans 12:1-2 ESV
I appeal to you therefore, brothers, by the mercies of God, to present your bodies as a living sacrifice holy and acceptable to God, which is your spiritual worship Do not be conformed to this world, but be transformed by the renewal of your mind, that by testing you may discern what is the will of God, what is good and acceptable and perfect.

Step 2: Discover and participate in each **challenge** with positive intent. Expect that each day you will discover something new about God and yourself that will help you understand the "right" job for you.

I will instruct you and teach you in the way you should go; I will counsel you and watch over you." Psalm 32:8 NIV

Step 3: Transform your words and thoughts by declaring out loud that what God has said to you is already done because it glorifies God. Even if you wake up on the wrong side of the bed, keep speaking God's truth.

Let the words of my mouth and the meditation of my heart be acceptable in your sight, O Lord, my rock and my redeemer.
Psalm 19:14

Step 4 : End each by responding to the following
- o   Did you do the challenge Yes or No?
- o   If no, why?
- o   If yes, what was the result?
- o   What did you learn?
- o   Read scripture again, give thanks, prayer and go to sleep

Success Tips:

1. *This is the no excuse zone… if it is difficult for you to start and end this way, then get up and prepare for bed 30 minutes earlier.*
2. *Keep this book and bible on your nightstand instead of your phone (don't start using apps if you get distracted easily). If you need to keep your phone near, then place it face down and put it on do not disturb.*
3. *In the beginning of the challenge reach out to your accountability partner after Gratitude and time with God (text or email).*
4. *If you need to keep your phone near you put it on "Do Not Disturb" when you are spending time with God in the morning.*
5. *Select a place in your house away from distractions to do morning routine.*
6. *Announce to family and friends that you are doing personal development, so you need to follow a schedule.*
7. *Celebrate small successes. For example, after the first three days celebrate your consistency.*
8. *Relax and Enjoy the process!*

CHAPTER *8*
Affirm & Declare

SOMETIMES IT'S EASY TO GET STUCK IN YOUR CURRENT **SITUATION and** convince yourself that this is as good as it gets. However, I am asking you to challenge every comfortable place in your life. In this book we are focusing on career navigation, but you need to consider your relationship with God, marriage, your family, your finances, and even your relationships with co-workers if you want to get Naked with God. Trust me all these relationships impact your ability to successfully navigate you career while getting naked with God.

God has better and greater for you! He is just waiting for you to see it and begin moving towards it. One of the first steps needed after you write your vision, is to affirm it. To affirm your vision, is to encourage yourself both mentally, physically, and 29verbally each day. For some of you that affirmation may nudge you to talk or dress in alignment with your future. Your affirmation may require for you to eat differently or work out as a part of the vision you wrote.

Create an Affirmation Wall of things you are declaring during your 21-day challenge. Things that make you feel great and things that you know will give God glory even though you don't know how it will happen.

Activity:

Each day touch the wall and declare that these things are going to happen during your private worship time. As things happen then you are going to rip that item down declare it is DONE and focus on the other items. Remember you do not have to continue to pray for things God has already done!

Share your affirmation wall with your accountability partner to make sure the items you have written are not about your agenda but allow you to discover things about yourself and will glorify God.

Do not be ashamed of your wall, talk about it and if someone sees your wall then speak in the tense of it is already done because it is God's hand. If it does not happen how you wrote it then know that it was not God's will and you might find yourself modifying words as you draw closer to God.

**You may want to take a picture or video of the wall to remind yourself of your affirmation during the day.*

After you are done creating your wall, write down how it makes you feel to see things that may have only been in your thoughts now they are in front of you?

Don't jump ahead STOP and in this book write down how you feel. Again, get Naked with God and jot down your feelings.

CHAPTER *9*
The 21-day challenge

HE TWENTY-ONE DAY CHALLENGE BEGINS, once you begin don't get discouraged and don't give up. If you start for a couple days and stop. Just jump right back into the challenges. Remember this is your journey so do not compare your progress to anyone else and remember the main goal in the process is what you hear from God and doing things that align with the word.

Psalms 119:105(NIV)
The Holy Spirit is such a gift from God. So, get started and allow his word to be a lamp to your feet and a light to your path.

CHALLENGE 1: WRITE THE VISION

Gratitude & Meditation (3 things you are grateful for)

1.____

2.____

3.____

Scripture: Habakkuk 2:2(NIV)
2 Then the LORD replied: "Write down the revelation and make it plain on tablets so that a herald may run with it.

Reflections

Challenge: *Capture your vision on paper. Think about what your life would look like if I honored God in every aspect. Do not over complicate this exercise. You can either create a vision on paper or you can open a document on your computer/tablet and create it with words and online images. Once you have created your vision place it somewhere you can always see it. You could take a picture from your phone and make it your screen saver.*

End of Day Recap

Did you do the challenge?   **YES**   **NO**

If no, why? (be honest and notify your accountability partner).

If yes, what was the result?

What did you learn?

Read scripture again, give thanks, prayer and go to sleep.
(Reminder let this be the last activity you do before going to bed).

CHALLENGE 2: PRIORITIES (values): what you say and what you do

Gratitude & Meditation (3 things you are grateful for)

1.____

2.____

3.____

Scripture: Matthew 6:33

"But seek first His kingdom and His righteousness, and all these things will be added to you.

Reflections

Challenge: *As a believer your priorities should be God, spouse, children, family and everything else. (if you are not married or do not have children then you would omit the categories you do not fall into.). However, you can recognize what is important or your values based on how you spend your time and money. The challenge for today is to look at your calendar (paper or digital) and look at your 3 months of your appointments in your calendar and bank statements. Record how much time you spent with God (praying and reading the word each day. How much time do you spend with your spouse and/or family? How did you spend your money was it on materialistic things compared to giving to others or tithes/offering to build up the kingdom of God?*

Getting Naked with God

End of Day Recap

Did you do the challenge?   YES   NO

If no, why? (be honest and notify your accountability partner).

If yes, what was the result?

What did you learn?

Read scripture again, give thanks, prayer and go to sleep.
(Reminder let this be the last activity you do before going to bed).

CHALLENGE 3: KNOWING YOUR WHY? (do your values line up with the word)

Gratitude & Meditation (3 things you are grateful for)

1.____

2.____

3.____

Scripture: Romans 12:2 ESV

Do not be conformed to this world, but be transformed by the renewal of your mind, that by testing you may discern what is the will of God, what is good and acceptable and perfect.

Reflections

Challenge: *Simon Sinek wrote a great book a few years ago, start with WHY? This concept of why we want or do things has become very popular keynote speeches and business environments, to be honest I even use this with my clients. This is such a simple question but can often be very difficult to answer if you do not spend a lot of time searching for purpose in life. I want you to get clarity on your why by using a technique called the 5 why's. Let me give you an illustration about how it works.*

Example of 5 whys general:

Why did you buy that car?

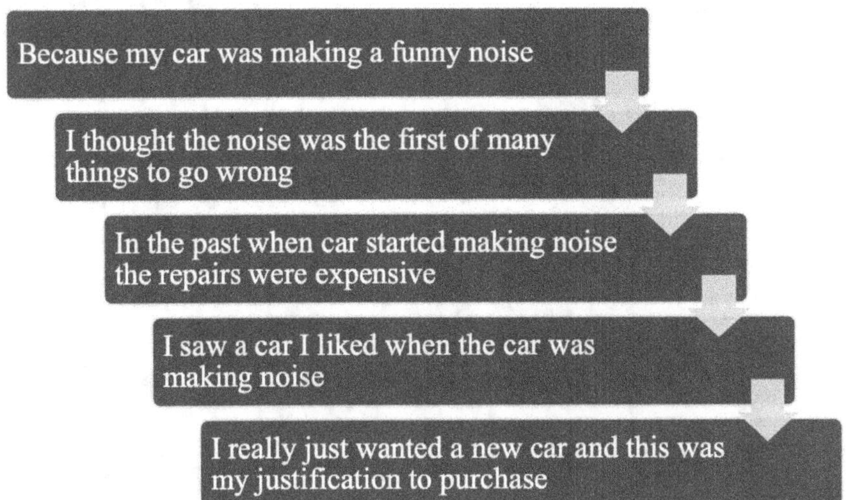

Example of 5 whys faith decision:

Why did you start your company?

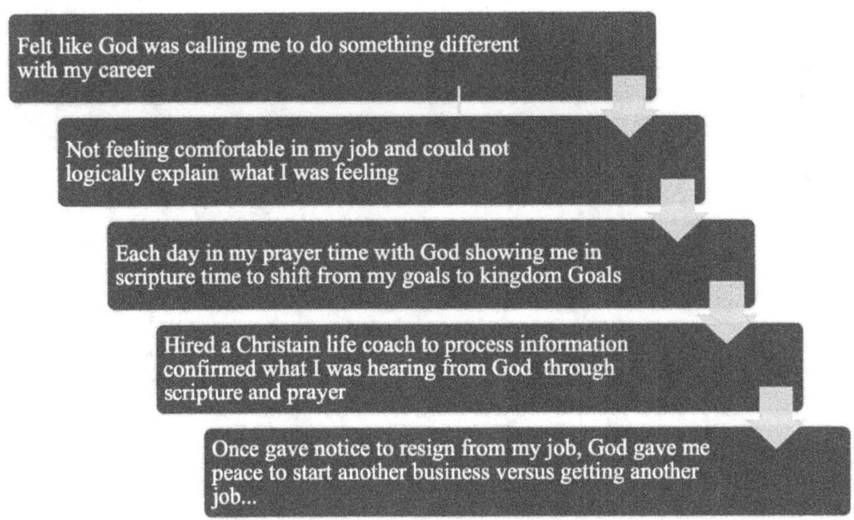

Your Turn:

Example of 5 whys general:

Why did you (fill in the blank________________)?

Example of 5 whys faith decision:

Why did you(fill in the blank________________)? (for example, get married,

change jobs, select church)

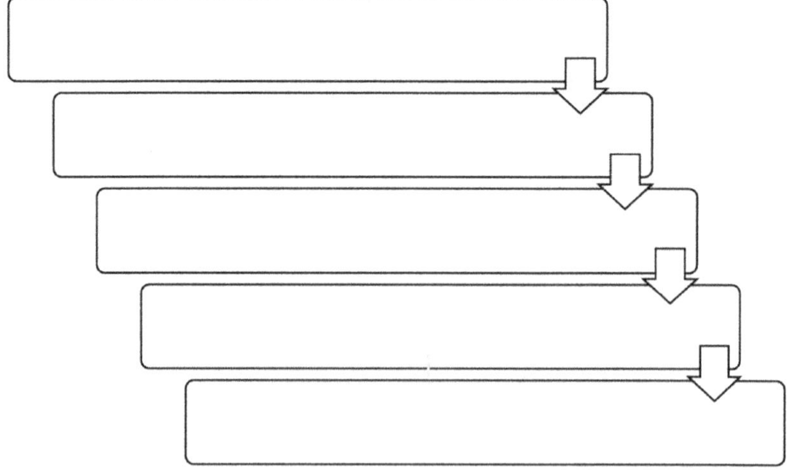

Additional Notes

End of Day Recap

Did you do the challenge?　　　YES　　　NO

If no, why? (be honest and notify your accountability partner).

If yes, what was the result?

What did you learn?

Read scripture again, give thanks, prayer and go to sleep. *(Reminder let this be the last activity you do before going to bed).*

CHALLENGE 4: TIME AND TASK *(why do I seem so busy and never enough time in a day no matter how hard I hustle)*

Gratitude & Meditation (3 things you are grateful for)

1.____

2.____

3.____

Scripture: Luke 12:34

For where your treasure is, there your heart will be also.

Reflections

Challenge: *I used to wear my superwoman cape as a badge of honor! I thought this is what successful people who loved the Lord did. However, as my responsibilities grew, meaning it wasn't just me anymore, I was married, then we had children, then I was serving at church, working full time, trying to be a good daughter, friend and co-worker. I thought this meant saying "no" was a bad word especially if I could help someone with their problem. However, what was the result? I was wasting a lot of time pleasing people (whether they wanted my help or not) and not honoring the relationships and responsibilities for the current season of my life. I use the word season often and basically it means where are you in life. What are* *my current responsibilities and what does God require of me? I knew what I was doing was not working because the most important relationship(marriage) was the last priority on my list. How did I discover this because?, I did a time and task analysis. I looked at how I spent my day versus my to do list and I quickly discovered WHY I didn't have time for the important things. Each morning I would wake up and because I didn't have a routine for my kids I would be running around and if someone called, I would shift my attention to them versus my kids. My husband worked midnights and my attitude was I will get to him when I see him, but I generally left the house before he got home from work. Once I finally made it to work instead of taking time to plan my day, I would walk around saying good morning and if one person was having a bad day, I felt like it was my duty to make their day better. The big question is how often did I ask my husband how his day was or more importantly what I was doing as a wife to help him have a good day.*

I no longer function that way at all I protect my time because it is precious. I do not believe in work life balance I believe we should prioritize our day based on the priorities in our life. Now it is your turn to do a time and task analysis. From the time you wake up until it is time to go to bed record EVERYTHING you did on a piece of paper or on a note on your phone. At the end of the day look at that list and ask yourself does what you did today focus on your faith and family? BE HONEST, although this is a single day challenge you might want to continue doing this for a couple of weeks to get a clearer picture.

LaTashia Martin

End of Day Recap

Did you do the challenge?   YES   NO

If no, why? (be honest and notify your accountability partner).

If yes, what was the result?

What did you learn?

Read scripture again, give thanks, prayer and go to sleep.
(Reminder let this be the last activity you do before going to bed).

CHALLENGE 5: ACCOUNTABILITY

Gratitude & Meditation (3 things you are grateful for)

1.____

2.____

3.____

Scripture:

Proverbs 27:17

17 As iron sharpens iron, so one person sharpens another.

Proverbs 15:22 ESV

22 Without counsel plans fail, but with many advisers they succeed.

Reflections

Challenge: This challenge takes vulnerability because asking someone to give you honest feedback and hold you accountable for doing what you said you would do can be difficult. What I have learned is to make progress with a plan you need accountability. When I began this work personally and helping other professionally people would want to hold themselves accountable with planning systems or other ways. I wasn't much better because I was so good at covering my real feelings and goals until I began spending more time with God. Spending time with God helped me realize just how much I needed people to hold me accountable. This was not an easy process and to be honest I still must work on this especially when I am working on goals that God has shown me that feel impossible by my own strength.

Now it is your turn, think about some of the areas that God has been showing you to do things differently. After you write an area down ask the Holy Spirit to either show you someone you know or create an opportunity for you to meet someone who can be your accountability person. It is important that you pray because this person needs to be firm in their word, and you must be able to receive from them.

In the beginning of the book we talked about having someone to keep you accountable for committing to the getting naked with God process. For this challenge I want you to go back to your original pledge and see if you have honored that commitment. If yes, then this challenge may not be as difficult. If you have not been checking in with your accountability person, I would suggest you start back up with this person. Then follow the same process with the area God revealed as you began reading today.

Do not rush this process but commit to the challenge.

What did you learn?

End of Day Recap

Did you do the challenge?   YES   NO

If no, why? (be honest and notify your accountability partner).

If yes, what was the result?

What did you learn?

Read scripture again, give thanks, prayer and go to sleep.
(Reminder let this be the last activity you do before going to bed).

CHALLENGE 6: SUPPORT GROUP

Gratitude & Meditation (3 things you are grateful for)

1.____

2.____

3.____

Scripture:

1 Thessalonians 5:11 ESV

Therefore encourage one another and build one another up, just as you are doing.

Reflections

Challenge: *In the previous challenge the focus was the importance of an accountability person. In this challenge I want to broaden our need for relationships for more than accountability. We need relationships for people to build us up and encourage us like the scripture says. In this challenge I want you to list 5 people who you have a relationship with that you encourage and lift each other up.*

When was the last time you have intentionally encouraged one or all of them? If it has been over a week then your challenge is to reach out to them by phone, in person and if you cannot do either write them a handwritten note (not an email or text).

Once you have encouraged and/or lifted them up take the flesh part out of it and what I mean that is you have zero expectation of a returned response no matter how big or little the gesture is. The key to this part of the challenge is to remember **Colossians 3:17(NIV)** *"And whatever you do, whether in word or deed, do it all in the name of the Lord Jesus, giving thanks to God the Father through him."*

The next part of today's challenge is for you to be brutally honest with yourself and ask when was the last time someone supported or checked in with you. Okay let me re-write, when was the last time you allowed someone to something kind to you. This can be hard to ask but be specific about what they did. A quote that was recently shared with me was from my chiropractor's grandmother Alice O'Neil, "receive the gift with the grace and honor the giver." This challenge is not about reciprocity it is about healthy, supportive relationships.

Who you have blessed? (not for bragging rights just to reflect)

Who blessed you?

Getting Naked with God

End of Day Recap

Did you do the challenge?   YES   NO

If no, why? (be honest and notify your accountability partner).

If yes, what was the result?

What did you learn?

Read scripture again, give thanks, prayer and go to sleep.
(Reminder let this be the last activity you do before going to bed).

CHALLENGE 7: REST AND REFLECT

Gratitude & Meditation (3 things you are grateful for)

1.____

2.____

3.____

Scripture:

Genesis 2:2-3:

2 By the seventh day God had finished the work he had been doing; so on the seventh day he rested from all his work. 3 Then God blessed the seventh day and made it holy, because on it he rested from all the work of creating that he had done.

Reflections

Challenge: *If you are the type of person who has a hard time relaxing and are always busy this might be the hardest challenge yet. The goal for today is to intentionally break away from everything and reset. I am not asking you to set yourself up for failure by relaxing the whole day but try to take a minimum of 2 hours to break away from all your normal business. Here is the key Jesus had the discipline to break away but most of us need to plan* *for success even on a day like this. To assist you with the rest and reflect challenge I would encourage you to schedule something to intentionally relax. For example, schedule time at a spa or pick up an old hobby. One thing I did on my relax and reflect days was crocheting. I choose to do something takes both hands for me to do it and put my phone on do not disturb. The more time I spent doing the work to rest and reflect the easier it has become. I no longer must schedule something to rest and relax I look forward to it.*

On days you rest and reflect I would suggest you begin to journal and spend time reading your bible. Taking this time will give you greater insight on who God created you to be and what he created you for. We serve a God who wants more for us than we often want for our self, but he is kind and patient. It is only when we take the time to rest and reflect that we can hear from him.

Give yourself a gift of time with God as you rest and reflect.

What did you do?

End of Day Recap

Did you do the challenge?   YES   NO

If no, why? (be honest and notify your accountability partner).

If yes, what was the result?

What did you learn?

Read scripture again, give thanks, prayer and go to sleep.
(Reminder let this be the last activity you do before going to bed).

CHALLENGE 8: ASK FOR HELP
Right Team, Right Terms, Right Now

Gratitude & Meditation (3 things you are grateful for)

1.______________________________________

2.______________________________________

3.______________________________________

Scripture:

Romans 12:5

In the same way, even though we are many individuals, Christ makes us one body and individuals who are connected to each other.

Reflections

Challenge: *For a long time when I was faced with a challenge, problem, project or most things if I was honest my first response was not to reach out to others. I would pride myself in going away in isolation to figure things out alone. However, my cover up is I would go to the passages in scripture when Jesus would go alone to pray (example Mark 1:35 or Luke 5:15-16). While there may be times that Holy Spirit may guide you to spend time in solitude the reality is that God made us to be in relationship with one another. We all have gifts and talents that help the body of Christ to be* *stronger. We also have gifts to support each other and God has shown me that we are better together.*

What I learned in the workplace and have applied to my life personally is that I don't have do everything if I want things to be done well. I also have learned that all help is not the right help for what I need. For example, when it comes to my children, if I need support beyond my mom. I only lean on support from friends and family that share my same values and views. This allows me to ask for help and I do not have to have long discussions about what is important to me.

As my family evolved, I had to make more intentional decisions around work and personal choices. I only took jobs that had flexibility and allowed to be present at all the things that were important to our family. I also had to learn to invest in resources that helped me live a life of intention. One thing you will hear me say is teamwork makes the dream work. The team of support that works for me may not work for you. The only way to have the right team is to be aware of your strengths and weaknesses.

The best part of team Martin is I am a big picture thinker while my husband focuses on today. He is also a man of routine and consistency while I am at the opposite end of the spectrum.

As I think about my closest friends and family, they know how important my faith and family are. Which means I don't have friends who cannot honor that if we are on the phone and one of kids needs me it is ok for me to hang up or put them on hold. Truth moment, it took me a while to do this consistently but that is where I am now.

Let's shift over to the workplace, again I am a big picture thinker but to successfully manage a team or hire the right support. You need to be self-aware and understand the resources you need to get the work done. I remember working all day and coming home with an attitude if I needed to prepare dinner or go to the grocery store. Years ago, I decided that I may not make dinner, but I can make dinner happen. This used to consist of eating out a lot but now with so many convenient stores to home options (grub hub, door dash, Instacart, pick up from Walmart or Target). Again, I tell people often I love how technology has allowed me to utilize some help with the push of a button.

What is my challenge to you? My challenge is to have you take time to reflect on what type of resources (the team) would help you have a better quality of life. How would that work for you? For example, instead of going grocery shopping you use Instacart. Instead of you doing all the errands with the kids you ask family or friends to help you.

Examine the people you spend the most time with, do they stress you out or you support each other. For the people who stress you put some boundaries on how much time you spend with them. Ask God to bring new people into your life.

Now write down a perfect day in the life of me....I would do the following and have support for(list out the items or support). How would they support you, under what terms?

This is a critical step in asking and accepting support. Pray for God to allow you to be NAKED during this exercise, for busy high capacity women this can be a challenge to ask for help. Now go do the WORK!

This challenge is about identifying help virtual, tech, or people. Do not proceed without "asking" people for help until the next challenge. You will learn how to manage by agreement.

List who would you ask to help you (home and work):

End of Day Recap

Did you do the challenge?   YES   NO

If no, why? (be honest and notify your accountability partner).

If yes, what was the result?

What did you learn?

Read scripture again, give thanks, prayer and go to sleep.
(Reminder let this be the last activity you do before going to bed).

CHALLENGE 9: MANAGE BY AGREEMENT

Gratitude & Meditation (3 things you are grateful for)

1.______________________________________

2.______________________________________

3.______________________________________

Scripture:

Exodus 18: 17-23 NIV

[17] Moses' fathers-in-law replied, "What you are doing is not good. [18] You and these people who come to you will only wear yourselves out. The work is too heavy for you; you cannot handle it alone. [19] Listen now to me and I will give you some advice, and may God be with you. You must be the people's representative before God and bring their disputes to him. [20] Teach them his decrees and instructions and show them the way they are to live and how they are to behave. [21] But select capable men from all the people—men who fear God, trustworthy men who hate dishonest gain—and appoint them as officials over thousands, hundreds, fifties and tens. [22] Have them serve as judges for the people at all times but have them bring every difficult case to you; the simple cases they can decide themselves. That will make your load lighter, because they will share it with you. [23] If you do this and God so commands, you will be able to stand the strain, and all these people will go home satisfied."

Reflections:

Challenge: *In the previous day you listed the type of team, terms and support you need. Whether it was a challenge or easy for you to list the type of support you need that part that could cause some discomfort is having an expectation conversation(s). A lesson I learned from one of my coaches is the importance of establishing expectations and managing to them. When you do not take this approach conflict can be based on emotions versus performance or what you need to be the best version of you.*

In the past when I have not managed by agreement I would pay for or accept help that was not helping. I remember hiring my first employee. I knew I had too much work for one person, but I did not have a clear objectives or tasks for my employee. I hired a great employee but didn't utilize the resource I was paying for. I knew this approach didn't work.

I went from a business hire for my side hustle to and hiring two employees at my regular job. My team expanded, I had more than enough help and tried to assign projects I thought they could complete without much assistance. Again "FAIL" because I thought I was clear about my expectations I didn't take enough time to evaluate the talent that was on my team beyond the interview.

I advise my small businesses to have a 90-day probation period where you can separate from employee without consequences or emotions when expectations are not met. I would recommend a similar approach for volunteers and people you pay for personal support like childcare, house cleaning, hairdresser, etc…

Where am I now? Currently no matter what type of help I am asking for personally or professionally I always clarify expectations and what "success" would look like. I share my form of communication style and take the time to understand the person's competencies and strengths.

I create tangible measurable goals and meet with person often to ensure expectations are being met on both sides (me and the employee/support). When things are going well, we move forward and when things are not going well, we discuss the issue in detail and decide the best way to move forward.

It has been much easier doing this in my professional life over personal life because at the end of the day your family is not disposable (and people shouldn't be either, but you can walk away). What I find works best in a work when dealing with work or business transactions is that you write our expectations, what success looks like, how and when you will work together, and best way to communicate. This may seem like a ton of effort, but it is the best way to work together well and no one is disappointed if things are just not a good "fit".

Now it is your turn, to help you out let me provide a template that you can use to manage by agreement. Don't start from scratch you would select someone from the people you listed in your "ask for help" challenge, pick someone new.

MANAGE BY AGREEMENT TEMPLATE

Project Description:
Responsible for managing social media to increase brand awareness. The goal is to grow social media following by 30% in the next 12 months.

List Task:
1. Decide which social media platforms are best for brand awareness.
2. Create a plan to post on top social media platform
3. Create a template for social media post and tracking results
4. Track the uploads and results
5. Meet every week to review the results

Manger expectations	Support expectations
√ Manager to send the information for social medial uploads every month √ Weekly check in to review results and uploads √ Provide feedback on performance and recommend feedback	√ Create template for social media post and tracking √ Upload weekly social media and send report to manger every week √ Make recommendations social based on tracking information √ Provide feedback on performance and recommend feedback

Dates	Results (define success)	Complete (Y)es or (N)o	Notes
x/xx/xxxx	Create a template for social media post and track results	Yes	
x/xx/xxxx	Upload 7 social media post on facebook each week	No	Upload post but didn't track results. Need to plan better

MANAGE BY AGREEMENT TEMPLATE

Project Description:	
List Task:	

Manger expectations	Support expectations

Dates	Results (define success)	Complete (Y)es or (N)o	Notes

Print name.   Date   Print name   Date

Signature   Date   Signature   Date

End of Day Recap

Did you do the challenge?   YES   NO

If no, why? (be honest and notify your accountability partner).

If yes, what was the result?

What did you learn?

Read scripture again, give thanks, prayer and go to sleep. *(Reminder let this be the last activity you do before going to bed).*

CHALLENGE 10: ANNOUNCE THE PLAN
Gratitude & Meditation (3 things you are grateful for)

1.____

2.____

3.____

Scripture:

Isaiah 55:11

So shall my word be that goes out from my mouth; it shall not return to me empty, but it shall accomplish that which I purpose, and shall succeed in the thing for which I sent it.

Reflections

Challenge: *Here is where things get real because you need to begin communicating your internal goals to different people in different ways. At this point you have made a commitment and are probably excited about the clarity because you have been getting naked with God. If you want to get people on board, you will not want to share the entire plan. This could be overwhelming and in the next chapter you will learn the baby steps to have everyone support the things you have discovered and written down.*

Here is your challenge, take a few minutes to think about everyone you will need to support your vision, hold you accountable, and support you to respond to what you have heard from God. After you have written down everyone you will need to reach out to. Take some time to reflect on your past interactions with them. Specifically, what has worked, what has not worked, and what was the hardest part of you interacting with these people. You also want to think about some of your successful conversations.

Don't just think about this take time to write this information down because in the next chapter you will take this information to approach everyone you have written down on the list. Taking this time will help you confirm the following:

1.   Did you include everyone?

2.   Have left people off the list that you may need to consider?

3.   Do you want to remove anyone?

End of Day Recap

Did you do the challenge?   YES   NO

If no, why? (be honest and notify your accountability partner).

If yes, what was the result?

What did you learn?

Read scripture again, give thanks, prayer and go to sleep.
(Reminder let this be the last activity you do before going to bed).

CHALLENGE 11: BABY STEPS
Gratitude & Meditation (3 things you are grateful for)

1.______________________________________

2.______________________________________

3.______________________________________

Scripture:

Luke 16:10 ESV

One who is faithful in a very little is also faithful in much, and one who is dishonest in a very little is also dishonest in much.

Reflections

Challenge: *Warning if you are a person who thinks of taking one step at a time already gives you anxiety. My ask is that you trust the process...which means please don't jump ahead without doing this challenge. It will be the foundation of shifting for a life of "I can do it myself" to partnering and collaborating with others so that you can all accomplish more together than separately. It will also help you spend time doing things that are your strength versus struggling to get stuff done alone.*

Living this way allows for more to get accomplished in less time and what you are doing could bless someone else to get inspired to do the same thing. Bonus is if you are partnering with an unbeliever and they might give getting naked with God a try because you are living your faith versus talking about it. So here we gooooo. As mentioned in the previous chapter your excitement about being naked with God can fill you with a lot enthusiasm which could have people move away versus joining you on the journey if you don't ease people into accepting the "new you".

Your challenge is to reach out to 1 or 2 people, just to ask to set up a meeting because you need their help. Don't move ahead of yourself at this point just set up the meeting.

Who are the 2 people?

When and how are you meeting with them?

End of Day Recap

Did you do the challenge?   YES   NO

If no, why? (be honest and notify your accountability partner).

If yes, what was the result?

What did you learn?

Read scripture again, give thanks, prayer and go to sleep.
(Reminder let this be the last activity you do before going to bed).

CHALLENGE 12: ASK MORE QUESTIONS

Gratitude & Meditation (3 things you are grateful for)

1.____

2.____

3.____

Scripture:

Jeremiah 33:3 ESV

Call to me and I will answer you and will tell you great and hidden things that you have not known.

Reflections

Challenge: *The challenge for today may seem simple but as you begin it can get complicated, especially for external processors. The challenge is before you respond to anyone's request or question with an answer try to ask at least three questions so that you better understand what they're asking before you respond either with an answer or a response to the request. For those of you who are good listeners and not external processors, this challenge may not be as difficult for you. Extroverts this challenge can be difficult.*

A book that I read a few years back is called the Question behind the Question by John Miller, if you struggle with this challenge I would encourage you to read this book and it will give you some great insight and some advantages on both why it's important to ask questions as well as how to ask good questions.

For today just stick to the basics go ahead with the skills and abilities that you have and begin asking questions before responding. During the day take some notes on what you learned by taking this approach, make sure you take time to reflect on how that experience felt.

What I learned from doing this is that often I was responding inappropriately to people because I didn't fully understand why they were asking for something. It has also saved me time because I didn't have to redo or start again due to lack of understanding.

How many times did you do ask more questions today?

How did it feel, be specific?

End of Day Recap

Did you do the challenge?   YES   NO

If no, why? (be honest and notify your accountability partner).

If yes, what was the result?

What did you learn?

Read scripture again, give thanks, prayer and go to sleep.
(Reminder let this be the last activity you do before going to bed).

CHALLENGE 13: WORK SMARTER NOT HARDER

Gratitude & Meditation (3 things you are grateful for)

1.____

2.____

3.____

Scripture:

Psalm 127:1-2(KJV)

Except the LORD build the house, they labor in vain that build it: except the LORD keep the city, the watchman waketh but in vain. It is vain for you to rise up early, to sit up late, to eat the bread of sorrows: for so he giveth his beloved sleep.

Reflections

Challenge: *Working harder not smarter could be a habit that we may not be aware we have created in our lives. The scripture challenges us to have discipline in how we approach work. For example, project planning should not take countless hours in isolation. Create a team before jumping into the work, having different perspectives can enhance not hinder your quality of life. I know these challenges are designed to be completed in a day so my challenge for you is to make sure before jumping into your day do the following:*

- *Create a to do list (if this is already a habit jump to next step)*
- *Evaluate how long each task should take and what time you would like to focus on it*
- *Ask yourself to do you need to complete the task or can you delegate it someone else (delegate early, delete from list and move on)*
- *If task requires attention to detail, then make sure you select a time that you will not have any interruptions*
- *Only focus on the work for the allotted time*
- *If you are unable to complete items on your list, ask yourself what will happen if I push them off until tomorrow or later date (then move them or complete them today)*
- *Create a work schedule and stick to it, in the beginning you may need to be flexible because you are not sure what works for you. As you get more disciplined with asking for help, you may be able to estimate the time required to do a task more accurately when someone else does it.*

Ready, Set, GOOOOOO for it…..

End of Day Recap

Did you do the challenge?   YES   NO

If no, why? (be honest and notify your accountability partner).

If yes, what was the result?

What did you learn?

Read scripture again, give thanks, prayer and go to sleep.
(Reminder let this be the last activity you do before going to bed).

CHALLENGE 14: REST AND REFLECT

Gratitude & Meditation (3 things you are grateful for)

1.____

2.____

3.____

Scripture:

Exodus 34:21 ESV

Six days you shall work, but on the seventh day you shall rest. In plowing time and in harvest you shall rest.

Reflections

Challenge: *Over the past several days getting naked with God to understand his vision for you and the priorities for this season of your life. If you have been doing the work, you might be a bit overwhelmed and are telling yourself, this stuff sounds great but there is no way I could possibly make time for all that God is showing me. Maybe you have been so busy doing the work you have not taken a moment to step back from the work to see trying to do it all alone is not helping you to accomplish anything. I get it honest I do! I cannot tell you how many great books I have plowed through taking copious notes with little or NO application. I was so busy completing the activities in the book but didn't have time to* *transition the words into actions in my life. If this is, you STOP READING. Put this book down and literally take a couple of cleansing breathes. If that does not help, then I want you to phone a friend and take a time out from this book and come back in couple of days with fresh perspective. Please let your accountability person know what you are doing and for how long so that you come back to this work. Getting naked with God is a process but even Jesus took a break to spend time with God and allowed his body to rejuvenate.*

Success tip…if you take time off be intentional and make "plans" for what you will do with your downtime. If not old habits or guilt of doing nothing might creep back in and you will fill up that space of rest with other things. Here is the kicker if someone calls you on your diversion tactics if you are strong willed like me you will not accept their candid feedback. Maybe you are not like me, but the point is making sure you take this time and inform your accountability person, so you return to the work of getting naked with God. Even if you are not overwhelmed you still should take today off.

What did you do to relax and how did it feel? *(Hopefully it was easier that the first time)*

End of Day Recap

Did you do the challenge?   YES   NO

If no, why? (be honest and notify your accountability partner).

If yes, what was the result?

What did you learn?

Read scripture again, give thanks, prayer and go to sleep.
(Reminder let this be the last activity you do before going to bed).

CHALLENGE 15: PLAN, PIVET PURPOSE

Gratitude & Meditation (3 things you are grateful for)

1.____

2.____

3.____

Scripture:

Isaiah 55:8-9 (NIV)

For my thoughts are not your thoughts, neither are your ways my ways, declares the LORD. For as the heavens are higher than the earth, so are my ways higher than your ways and my thoughts than your thoughts.

Reflections

Challenge: *In this passage of scripture the focus is on how God just thinks differently than us. Although the bible does shows us attributes of God and we are made in the image of Christ once we are saved. We still cannot think or respond exactly like God does and this can hinder our ability and limit the capabilities of what God can do in and through us. Your challenge for today is to sit quietly and reflect on 3 situations that happened within the last couple of weeks. Write them in the first column, in the second column write your plan or how you were going to approach the* *situation, in the third column write what happened and how you saw a move a God in the situation.*

You might be asking why I am having you do this exercise? The purpose is to understand that we might have plans be we always want to be open to how God guides us with the Holy Spirit. If you go a little deeper with this challenge, in the second column did you consider what scripture said you should respond, or did you make decision without considering God?

Moving forward as you create plans always allow room for the Holy Spirit to guide your decision. If something doesn't "feel" right or things do not go according to your plan pause and Pray before moving forward.

Final tip, expect God to show up and interrupt your plans and when he does just say thank you Lord. What will you have me to do? Surrender with a smile makes the whole experience better.

Situation	Your Plan	What happen, did you experience a move of God?

End of Day Recap

Did you do the challenge?   **YES**   **NO**

If no, why? (be honest and notify your accountability partner).

If yes, what was the result?

What did you learn?

Read scripture again, give thanks, prayer and go to sleep.
(Reminder let this be the last activity you do before going to bed).

CHALLENGE 16: DELEGATE
(doing work differently)

Gratitude & Meditation (3 things you are grateful for)

1.____

2.____

3.____

Scripture:
Exodus 18:17-27 (NIV)

[17] Moses' fathers-in-law replied, "What you are doing is not good. [18] You and these people who come to you will only wear yourselves out. The work is too heavy for you; you cannot handle it alone. [19] Listen now to me and I will give you some advice, and may God be with you. You must be the people's representative before God and bring their disputes to him. [20] Teach them his decrees and instructions and show them the way they are to live and how they are to behave. [21] But select capable men from all the people—men who fear God, trustworthy men who hate dishonest gain—and appoint them as officials over thousands, hundreds, fifties and tens. [22] Have them serve as judges for the people at all times but have them bring every difficult case to you; the simple cases they can decide themselves. That will make your load lighter, because they will share it with you. [23] If you do this and God so commands, you will be able to stand the strain, and all these people will go home satisfied."

24 Moses listened to his father-in-law and did everything he said. 25 He chose capable men from all Israel and made them leaders of the people, officials over thousands, hundreds, fifties and tens. 26 They served as judges for the people at all times. The difficult cases they brought to Moses, but the simple ones they decided themselves.

27 Then Moses sent his father-in-law on his way, and Jethro returned to his own country

Reflections

Challenge: *If you have the type of personality where you need to be in control you may find this challenge to be extremely difficult. It is important that you realize the importance of working with others in your family, with your friends and at work. To be successful, whom ever you choose to help you with this challenge I would advise you to let them know that you understand that the request is out of character for you. Don't over think, keep it simple by going back to Challenge 8 where you have already listed people you like to help from. The goal is to* **DELEGATE**.

The challenge is for you ask someone for help on a task that you currently do not enjoy. Give them instructions and expectations, confirm they understand then step away. If they have questions, they must reach out to you, but you are NOT allowed to reach out to them. Agree on a completion date and what success would look like.

After you have assigned the task to someone step away and reflect on how the experience felt by responding to the questions below:

- How hard was it for you to identify something to delegate on a scale from 1(easy) to 5(hard).__________________________
- Write a few sentences how it felt asking for help __________

  ____

  ____

  ____

  ____

- Throughout the day were you able to let the person complete the task without you checking in? YES or NO

- When the person completed the task, did they meet your expectation? YES   OR   NO

- Will you continue to seek additional opportunities to ask for help? YES OR   NO

- Any other emotions that you would like to capture for this challenge

End of Day Recap

Did you do the challenge?   **YES**   **NO**

If no, why? (be honest and notify your accountability partner).

If yes, what was the result?

What did you learn?

Read scripture again, give thanks, prayer and go to sleep.
(Reminder let this be the last activity you do before going to bed).

CHALLENGE 17: CREATE THE PLAN

Gratitude & Meditation (3 things you are grateful for)

1.____

2.____

3.____

Scripture:

Proverbs 16:3 ESV

Commit your work to the Lord, and your plans will be established.

Reflections

Challenge: *Most mornings I wake up and create a to do list. In the past I would not always understand that the things on my to do list are merely task and without some thought I still many not accomplish my goals. The challenge for today will go beyond the standard to do list and connect it to something bigger. It is the bigger that you can pray to God to help you accomplish.*

Think about a task you just cannot seem to accomplish or complete. Perhaps it is because you are approaching the task without context. The STAR method is a great way to put things in perspective and help you accomplish goals and tasks.

*STAR is an acronym for **S**ituation **T**ask **A**ction and **R**esults this is an easy way to create a simple plan. Below is a template you can use to use the STAR method.*
Begin with the situation:

Example situation, I *want my family to help me with household chores.*

STAR METHOD:

SITUATION	Currently I do all of the household chores and I went back to work so I cannot keep up with all of responsibilities at home and work. I have not asked for help in the past.
TASK	<ul><li>Need to ask for help from my husband and children.</li><li>Create a chore chart template</li><li>Meet with family to discuss situation and ask for their help</li><li>Fill in the chore chart</li></ul>
ACTION	Family agrees to help me household chores
RESULTS	Family helps with household chores and I am not overwhelmed and frustrated

YOUR TURN:
What is the situation?

STAR MODEL

SITUATION	
TASK	
ACTION	
RESULS	

End of Day Recap

Did you do the challenge?   **YES**   **NO**

If no, why? (be honest and notify your accountability partner).

If yes, what was the result?

What did you learn?

Read scripture again, give thanks, prayer and go to sleep.
(Reminder let this be the last activity you do before going to bed).

CHALLENGE 18: ACTIVATE THE PLAN
Gratitude & Meditation (3 things you are grateful for)

1.____

2.____

3.____

Scripture:

Proverbs 21:5 ESV

The plans of the diligent lead surely to abundance, but everyone who is hasty comes only to poverty.

Reflections

Challenge: *In the previous challenge you learned about the STAR method to create a plan. I cannot tell you the number of plans I have created and to be honest that is as far as they went. I wrote plans but did not connect any specific goals around the plan. So, I would not activate the plan. In this scripture when it says, "plans of the diligent", what that has meant for me is I needed to activate the plan.*

*Creating goals is taking the **T** step in the STAR method to activate the plan. I know I am throwing a lot of acronyms your way, but the key is BABY STEPS take your time and go at your own pace.*

*To create goals, it is important that they are SMART (**S**pecific, **M**easurable, **A**ttainable, **R**ealistic, and **T**imebound). I* *will provide an example using the situation from the previous challenge.*

    The previous situation: <u>I want my family to help me with household chores.</u> In the star method I am going to select ONE <u>T</u>ask and create a SMART goal. The task I am selecting is create a template for chore chart.

Example of a SMART goal is: *I will create a chore chart template in Microsoft excel by March 10th.*

Confirm your goal I SMART by responding to each statement.
- √   **Specific:** Create a chore chart
- √   **Measurable:** Did you create chore chart by March 10th
- √   **Attainable:** I have Microsoft excel and know how to create chart, so it is attainable
- √   **Realistic:** It is realistic because I can create it by myself on my laptop
- √   **Timebound:** Timebound will have it completed by March 10th.

Your Turn:
Write out your SMART goal:_

Is it SMART?
- √   **Specific:**

- √   **Measurable:**

- √   **Attainable:**

- √   **Realistic:**

- √   **Timebound:**

End of Day Recap

Did you do the challenge?   **YES**   **NO**

If no, why? (be honest and notify your accountability partner).

If yes, what was the result?

What did you learn?

Read scripture again, give thanks, prayer and go to sleep. *(Reminder let this be the last activity you do before going to bed).*

CHALLENGE 19: EVALUATE

Gratitude & Meditation (3 things you are grateful for)

1.____

2.____

3.____

Scripture:

Luke 14:28 28

"Suppose one of you wants to build a tower. Won't you first sit down and estimate the cost to see if you have enough money to complete it? 29 For if you lay the foundation and are not able to finish it, everyone who sees it will ridicule you, 30 saying, 'This person began to build and wasn't able to finish.

Reflections

Challenge: *When was the last time you sat back and reflected on how things are going? I have met so many people who say life is going great or they are not sure what I mean, or they are just not happy. By now you are probably aware that before jumping to conclusions I ask lots of questions. I am no different in this area when it comes to measuring plans, quality of life etc....*

The interesting thing is when I talk about measuring success it is not always about taking a count for something like, how much you weigh, how much money you have in the bank, how many of....you name it. Not saying you will not have to measure something this way, but it is not the only way to evaluate progress.

Evaluating is a check in to ensure that what you are doing is having an impact on you being the best version of you based on how God has designed us to live. The key is that you are measuring your impact based on what the word says we should be not just our own goals that are not helping to form us more and more in his image.

I will try not to complicate this process. There are two ways to measure one is based on qualitative impact and the other is quantitative results. In this challenge I would like you to evaluate both types as it relates to what you have learned by getting naked with GOD while completing these challenges.

Before I give you some ideas on how to evaluate how things are going let me provide more information on the two types.

"**Quantitative data** is statistical and is typically structured in nature – meaning it is more rigid and defined. This type of data is measured using numbers and values, which makes it a more suitable candidate for data analysis"

Example: I want to read my bible for 15 minutes 5 days per week.

Quantitative measure tool example:

Day of the Week	Sun	Mon	Tue	Wed	Thur	Fri	Sat	Total number of "Y"
Did I read bible for 15 min. (Y)es or (N)o	Y	Y	N	Y	N	N	Y	4

Qualitative data is non-statistical and is typically unstructured or semi-structured in nature. This data isn't necessarily measured using hard numbers used to develop graphs and charts. Instead, it is categorized based on properties, attributes, labels, and other identifiers."

Qualitative data evaluation process:
Example: Certain music makes me feel happy and I wonder why?
Steps:
- √ After listening to music, I will create a reflective journal entry when music makes me happy over the next month (not every day just when I hear music that makes me happy).
- √ At the end of the month, review the journal entry and identify themes that I associated with music.
- √ Summarize what you learned.

Your turn…select the type of evaluation you would like to do and as you are thinking about this challenge ask yourself. What can I do with the information I learn during this evaluation? The purpose of collecting information just for the sake of collecting information is not beneficial. Use what you learn to help you improve in the area you collected.

I am not providing a template because this challenge is based on what you want to focus on. Remember your context of getting naked with God, evaluate based on what you are trying to discover about your experience with getting naked with God. In the space below summarize what you have learned about yourself as you have gone through the get Naked with God challenge.

Evaluation is not a one-time experience; you want to check in to ensure you that you do not slip back into old habits. The key is it is important to evaluate your progress no matter what because the world is constantly changing. You will need to continue to get naked with God to ensure you maintain the things you have taken so much time to learn.

Document below how you will continue measure your progress.

End of Day Recap

Did you do the challenge?   YES   NO

If no, why? (be honest and notify your accountability partner).

If yes, what was the result?

What did you learn?

Read scripture again, give thanks, prayer and go to sleep.
(Reminder let this be the last activity you do before going to bed).

CHALLENGE 20: REVISE

Gratitude & Meditation (3 things you are grateful for)

1.____

2.____

3.____

Scripture:

Proverbs 19:21 ESV

Many are the plans in the mind of a man, but it is the purpose of the Lord that will stand.

Reflections

Challenge: *In many of the challenges, your ideas and approaches may have seemed like a great idea but as you spent time asking God for wisdom you may have discovered that you should have considered other things. This is totally natural; the question is when you were shown something different how did you respond? Were you busy just trying to complete the challenge or did you take time to respond to the voice of God?*

I love this scripture because I cannot tell you how many times, I had a plan, but God had a purpose for my outcomes to be different than I anticipated.

During today's challenge I would like you to think back to all the challenges you completed and ask God how you could have approached the task differently. If it is hard for you to hear from God, then take time to reflect on challenges and pray for God to reveal something to you. You may not have an answer immediately, be patient, don't force this experience.

Once you receive an answer from God, go back and do the challenge again and reflect on the results.

Capture Them Here:

End of Day Recap

Did you do the challenge?   **YES**   **NO**

If no, why? (be honest and notify your accountability partner).

If yes, what was the result?

What did you learn?

Read scripture again, give thanks, prayer and go to sleep.
(Reminder let this be the last activity you do before going to bed).

CHALLENGE 21: REST, REFLECT & RE-ENTER

Gratitude & Meditation (3 things you are grateful for)

1.____

2.____

3.____

Scripture:

2 Corinthians 5:17 (NIV)

17 Therefore, if anyone is in Christ, the new creation has come:[a] The old has gone, the new is here!

Hebrews 4:9-11 (NIV)

There remains, then, a Sabbath-rest for the people of God; for anyone who enters God's rest also rests from his own work, just as God did from his. Let us, therefore, make every effort to enter that rest, so that no one will fall by following their example of disobedience.

Reflections

Challenge: *Congratulations! You have just participated in multiple challenges that required you to intentionally get naked with GOD. The purpose for the challenges were tangible ways that you could* *reflect on who you are, approach life differently and have some candid conversation with God. If you took the time to do a challenge every day that was a lot of time and commitment. My challenge for you today is for you to write down a way to rest and celebrate your hard work.*

This book is not written in a way that you will ever finish it but today the challenge is for you to CELEBRATE! CELEBRATE! CELEBRATE!

Write it down and make it happen…..

- **How will you REST………**

- **How and when will you celebrate…….**

End of Day Recap

Did you do the challenge?   YES   NO

If no, why? (be honest and notify your accountability partner).

If yes, what was the result?

What did you learn?

Read scripture again, give thanks, prayer and go to sleep.
(Reminder let this be the last activity you do before going to bed).

CHAPTER *10*
Re-entry

CONGRATULATIONS!, You have taken time to focus on yourself. You have intentionally heard from God while participating in each of these challenges. Now, I know that many of these activities may have seemed awkward at the time, but let's take a moment to reflect on what you have learned and create a strategy for ongoing success.

This process is called re-entry it may feel unnecessary, but the reality is if you want sustainable success this is the most important part of the process if you want to continue to allow God to mold and shape you in his image.

Before creating your re-entry plan it is important to acknowledge that this was a personal journey and it was YOUR experience. Although you have changed people around you, unless you read the book together, have not.   It is not their fault if they keep treating you like they did before this experience.

The best way to re-enter is reteach people how to treat you. In the beginning it can be challenging because until this point they are responding based on who they have known you to be. Do not get frustrated just continue to get naked with God and ask him for wisdom as you are responding *(use some of the challenges to help you)*.

Emotional responses are never good, it is more about responding based on who God created you to be and using scripture to respond in ways that glorify God.

The more you do this the more people will modify how they treat you and that can be uncomfortable too. In your discomfort good or bad ask God to give you enough confidence in him to respond in LOVE.

About the Author

LaTashia M. Martin has a passion for coaching busy professionals and small business owners to discover their authentic selves. She is an excellent communicator, creative problem-solver and motivator for both individuals and teams. As an Organizational Development practitioner, she has a proven track record.

LaTashia excels at career mapping, teambuilding, organizational leadership development, effective com munication, HR analytics, performance and succession management, and training for all levels of employment.

LaTashia the owner of VonSwy Solutions an organizational development and training company that focuses on career pathing and leadership training. LaTashia is a certified Lean Six Sigma and Lean Black Belt professional who combines her engineering and HR experience to create strategic solutions with measurable results in a way for her clients to accomplish their goal. She is a Certified Career Coach, DiSC & MBTI, Certified.

She has a BS in Engineering from Rochester Institute of Technology and MS in Organizational Development and Communication from Canisius College. Her greatest accomplishment is being a wife of 22 years and the mom of 3 children.

www.latashiamartin.com

APPENDIX

REFLECTIVE JOURNALING

Goal of this assignment Our goal for reflective journaling is to take a holistic look at your business and life. What I have experienced with many of my business owners is how they handle situations at home is not much different then how they handle situations as a business owner. Trust the process and be honest. When we meet as a group you only have to share to your level of comfort.

What is it? Reflective journals are personal records of learning experiences. Typically, you are asked to record an experience just after it occurs. Entries in journals and learning logs can be prompted by questions about a problem, situation, or your thought processes about what happened at a particular time. Journals and learning logs are used to prompt a coaching session.

Method of Creating Reflective Journals and Learning Logs It is suggested that you capture all formal and informal events which will prove useful when the time comes to return to the reflective journal or learning log for review. Focus on the areas which pose the most problems or difficulty in addition to those which are less problematic. Key to reflective journals and learning logs is to be honest about what you are experiencing and real emotions and feelings.

Before you start reflective journaling?
Materials
Both paper-based and online journals or logs can be effective, but I would suggest getting a little notebook that you can keep with you, something about writing down have a different effect. Definitely keep it on your nightstand it seems like ideas will come to you at the oddest times after you had an experience you journaled about earlier.

Mindset Shift Pre-work
Go to a quite spot where you can honestly describe your business not in its current state but how you imagine things running in a "Perfect" world. What your role would be, what type of clients you service, and what is your "dream team". Write this vision without any constraints, financial, time, access to resources. Try to write without interruption for at least 15 minutes.

Ok now it is time to get to work…
As you go through your day try to be aware of your emotions specifically as it relates to you running your business how you journaled in the pre-work. If you have a great experience write it down and if you have a negative experience write it down (personal and professional). Do not approach this type of journaling as something you need to do for any specific amount of frequency. Quality is more important than quantity.

Reflective Journaling
Step 1. "Write, record"
• Document the experience with as many details as possible.
• Who was involved with the situation?
• What did they have to do with the situation?

Step 2. Reflect, think about
• What are your reactions?
• What are your feelings?
• What are the good and the bad aspects of the situation?
• What you have learned?

PAUSE… you don't have to go any further we can use the information below for our goal setting meeting. But it is your choice.

Step 3. Analyze, explain, gain insight
• What was really going on?
• What sense can you make of the situation?
• Can you demonstrate an improved awareness and self-development because of the situation?

Step 4. Conclusions
• What can be concluded in a general and specific sense from this
• situation/experience and the analyses you have undertaken?

Step 5. Personal action plan
• What are you going to do differently in this type of situation next time?
• What steps are you going to take on the basis of what you have learned?"

Summary
• Reflective journals and learning logs can be useful as a teaching and learning tool. Either format can be adopted in any discipline where you can determine

Key to reflective journals and learning logs is to see progression over a period and to "gain a sense of achievement.

Additional Notes

www.ingramcontent.com/pod-product-compliance
Lightning Source LLC
Chambersburg PA
CBHW070844250726
48662CB00003B/1359